FAMOUS PEOPLE
FAMOUS LIVES

Biographies of famous people to
support the curriculum.

Cleopatra

by Harriet Castor
Illustrations by Richard Morgan

W
FRANKLIN WATTS
NEW YORK•LONDON•SYDNEY

First published in 1999 by
Franklin Watts
96 Leonard Street
London
EC2A 4XD

Franklin Watts Australia
14 Mars Road
Lane Cove
NSW 2066

ISBN: 0 7496 3531 2

A CIP catalogue record for this book is
available from the British Library.

Dewey Decimal Classification Number: 932

10 9 8 7 6 5 4 3 2 1

Series editor: Sarah Ridley
History consultant: Dr Anne Millard

Printed in Great Britain

Cleopatra

More than 2,000 years ago, a
little girl lived with her sisters and
brothers in a large palace
in Alexandria, Egypt. The little
girl was a princess, and her
name was Cleopatra.

At that time Egypt's royal
family wasn't Egyptian, but
Greek. They were called the
Ptolemies. Cleopatra's father,
Ptolemy XII, was the king.

Egypt was a rich country, but it wasn't peaceful. Many people didn't like having a Greek king. When Cleopatra was twelve, there was so much trouble that her father had to run away.

Ptolemy went to Rome to ask for help. Rome was the most powerful place in the world at that time. Its armies had conquered many countries and turned them into a massive Roman empire.

All right, we'll help. But you will have to pay us first.

While Ptolemy was away, his eldest daughter declared herself Queen of Egypt. The Romans agreed to send soldiers to help make Ptolemy king again.

By the time Ptolemy got back to Egypt, his eldest daughter had been murdered. His second daughter, Berenice, had made herself queen. With the help of Roman soldiers, Ptolemy took control. Berenice was executed.

Cleopatra was now next in line to the throne. She had already learnt that ruling Egypt was a difficult and dangerous job.

When Cleopatra was eighteen, her father died. Egyptian tradition said that a woman wasn't allowed to rule by herself. So Cleopatra became queen and her eldest brother became King Ptolemy XIII.

Tradition also said that brothers and sisters who were kings and queens should marry each other. So, after a while, they did.

For now, because Ptolemy was only ten, Cleopatra had to rule jointly with his advisers. The most powerful of them was called Photinus. He and Cleopatra hated each other.

Photinus tried to push Cleopatra off the throne, so that her brother could rule alone. Cleopatra and Photinus both gathered armies, and got ready to fight.

Just then Julius Caesar, the ruler
of the Roman Empire, arrived
in Egypt. He summoned
Cleopatra, Photinus and young
Ptolemy to a meeting at the
royal palace.

Cleopatra thought of a good way to get Caesar on her side: she became Caesar's lover. Caesar said Ptolemy must not be king alone; he must rule with Cleopatra. Photinus and Ptolemy were furious.

Photinus and Ptolemy sent secret messages, ordering their army to attack Alexandria. When Caesar found out, he had Photinus executed. Ptolemy escaped, and there was a battle between his army and Caesar's army. Caesar's won. Ptolemy was found dead in the River Nile.

Cleopatra still wasn't allowed to rule alone, so she married her youngest brother, who became King Ptolemy XIV.

In triumph, Cleopatra and
Caesar sailed up the River Nile.
Then Caesar went back to
Rome. Soon, Cleopatra joined
him there. She brought her new
baby, who was Caesar's son.
He was nicknamed Caesarion.

Cleopatra stayed in Rome for over a year, ruling Egypt from a distance. But then Caesar was murdered by his enemies. Cleopatra sailed back to Egypt.

There, Cleopatra's brother died. It's possible she had him killed. She made Caesarion king in his place.

Ruling Egypt was a difficult job, but Cleopatra was good at it. She kept the peace. She dealt cleverly with foreign powers.

The most important power was Rome. Now Caesar was dead, two groups of Roman leaders were fighting to take over. Both groups asked Cleopatra for help.

Cleopatra pretended to each group that she was about to help. In fact she was waiting to see who won.

The winners were called Octavian and Mark Antony. They decided to rule half the Roman Empire each.

Octavian took the west and Antony took the east.

Because the Romans were so powerful, Cleopatra needed to make Antony her friend.

When Antony called Cleopatra
to a meeting, they became not
just friends, but lovers. They
also did some hard bargaining.
Antony wanted money.
Cleopatra wanted help
against her enemies.

For a while Antony lived in Alexandria. He was impressed by Cleopatra's magnificent court, by Alexandria's famous museum and its lighthouse.

Then Antony left, and was away for three years. When he and Cleopatra met again, it was because he needed money. Cleopatra made Antony give back land that had been taken from Egypt. In return she promised to build him ships.

Cleopatra wanted Antony to stay with her, so that they could be the most powerful couple in the world, ruling all their lands together.

Antony had a wife in Rome:
Octavian's sister. But Antony
and Octavian had never really
been friends. Octavian kept
telling everyone in Rome that
he was a much better ruler
than Antony.

Antony decided to divorce his wife and stay with Cleopatra. Now he and Octavian weren't friends at all – they were enemies.

Cleopatra and Antony held
a magnificent celebration in
Alexandria. They sat side by
side on golden thrones, on a
silver platform. By now, they
had had three children together.

Antony announced that he was giving each one a kingdom.
He also said that Caesarion was Caesar's proper heir. This meant he wanted Caesarion to take Octavian's place.

Cleopatra and Antony began to prepare for war against Octavian. They set up their first headquarters at Ephesus, in a part of Antony's lands called Asia Minor. Some important Romans joined them there.

Cleopatra attended every
meeting. Some of the Romans
didn't like this. They wanted
Cleopatra to go home.
But Cleopatra refused.
Octavian knew that many
Romans hated Cleopatra.

So Octavian didn't declare war
on Antony – he declared war on
Cleopatra.

Octavian set off with his army and navy. Between them, they trapped Cleopatra and Antony at a place called Actium. There was a big battle. Cleopatra and Antony lost many ships and had to leave much of Antony's army.

They sailed back to Egypt.
Antony was very depressed.
Cleopatra made plans to
leave Egypt.

Cleopatra told Caesarion to set off first. Intending to follow him, she had ships dragged across the desert from the River Nile to the Red Sea. But when the ships got to the sea, Cleopatra's enemies set them on fire.

All Cleopatra and Antony could do was wait for Octavian. They sent him messages. Cleopatra offered to give up her throne if Octavian would let her children rule Egypt instead. Antony offered to kill himself if Octavian would spare Cleopatra.

Cleopatra had ordered a magnificent tomb to be built for her. Now she shut herself inside it, with all her treasure.

Antony thought Cleopatra was dead, so he stabbed himself. Cleopatra heard about it, and sent for him. As he was dying, Antony was carried to her tomb. The doors were sealed so he was passed in through a window. Inside, Antony died.

We've got to get that treasure.

Octavian had arrived in Egypt. He wanted Cleopatra's treasure. He sent a team of men to get it: one distracted Cleopatra while the others burst in.

Octavian made Egypt part of his Roman empire. He told Cleopatra that he was going to take her to Rome. He said he would parade her and her children through the streets as prisoners.

Cleopatra was horrified. She decided she would rather die than let this happen.

Cleopatra poisoned herself. She was found dead on a golden couch, dressed in her royal robes.

Most people think Cleopatra was bitten by a poisonous snake. Some said she scratched herself with a poisoned hair-pin or comb, or used a poisoned ointment.

Further facts

Can we be sure?

It is difficult to be sure exactly what happened in Cleopatra's lifetime. Very little survives that was written by anyone who was alive then. Most of the people who wrote about her later were Octavian's supporters. They saw Cleopatra as a wicked enemy. They didn't mention that she was a clever, capable and energetic ruler.

The Roman Empire

The Roman Empire was massive. At its biggest, nearly 150 years after Cleopatra's death, it included most of modern Europe, the north coast of Africa, modern Turkey, Syria, Israel and parts of modern Egypt and Iraq.

Kings, queens and consuls

Rome was a republic. This meant that it wasn't ruled by a monarch (a king or queen). Instead it had leaders called consuls, who were supposed to be elected every year. One of the reasons why the Romans hated Cleopatra was that she was a queen, and they were worried that, under her influence, a monarchy might be set up in Rome. After Cleopatra's death, though, Octavian became the first Roman emperor, and was as powerful as any king. He was known as the Emperor Augustus.

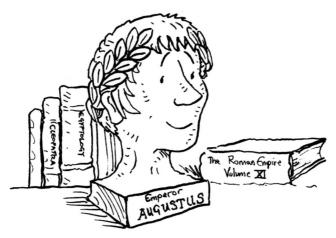

Some important dates in Cleopatra's lifetime

70 or 69 BC Cleopatra is born, the third daughter of Ptolemy XII, King of Egypt.

58 BC Ptolemy flees to Rome. His eldest daughter takes the throne as Queen Cleopatra VI.

55 BC Ptolemy XII becomes king again, with Roman help.

51 BC Ptolemy XII dies. Cleopatra becomes Queen Cleopatra VII, ruling jointly with her brother, King Ptolemy XIII.

48 BC Julius Caesar arrives in Egypt. He restores Cleopatra to the throne, alongside her brother.

46 BC Cleopatra joins Caesar in Rome, with her youngest brother, now King Ptolemy XIV.

44 BC Caesar is murdered – Cleopatra and Ptolemy XIV return to Egypt. Ptolemy soon dies. Caesarion becomes Ptolemy XV Caesar.

41 BC Mark Antony summons Cleopatra to a meeting at Tarsus, now in Turkey.

34 BC Cleopatra and Antony hold a magnificent celebration.

32 BC Two Roman consuls and between two and three hundred Roman senators leave Italy to join Antony and Cleopatra.

31 BC The Battle of Actium. Octavian wins, but Cleopatra and Antony escape to Egypt.

30 BC Antony and Cleopatra kill themselves.